Lerner SPORTS ROOKIE

SOCCER MANIA

BEST WOMEN'S SOCCER PLAYERS

Cara Krenn

Lerner Publications ◆ Minneapolis

For Kelly & Caroline

Lerner Publications Company
An imprint of Lerner Publishing Group, Inc.
241 First Avenue North
Minneapolis, MN 55401 USA

For reading levels and more information, look up this title at www.lernerbooks.com.

Main body text set in Mikado. Typeface provided by HVD fonts.

Editor: Evan Villas **Designer:** Viet Chu
Lerner team: Sue Marquis

Library of Congress Cataloging-in-Publication Data

Names: Krenn, Cara, author.
Title: Best women's soccer players / Cara Krenn.
Description: Minneapolis, MN : Lerner Publications, [2026] | Series: Soccer mania (Lerner sports rookie) | Includes bibliographical references and index. | Audience: Ages 5-8 | Audience: Grades K-1 | Summary: "She shoots, she scores! Readers discover extraordinary athletes and their remarkable achievements in the world of women's soccer"— Provided by publisher.
Identifiers: LCCN 2024037182 (print) | LCCN 2024037183 (ebook) | ISBN 9798765668375 (library binding) | ISBN 9798765683736 (paperback) | ISBN 9798765681091 (epub)
Subjects: LCSH: Women soccer players—Biography—Juvenile literature. | Soccer players—Biography—Juvenile literature. | Soccer—Juvenile literature.
Classification: LCC GV942.7.A1 K75 2026 (print) | LCC GV942.7.A1 (ebook) | DDC 796.3340922 [B]—dc23/eng/2024813

LC record available at https://lccn.loc.gov/2024037182
LC ebook record available at https://lccn.loc.gov/2024037183

Manufactured in the United States of America
1-1011708-53805-12/13/2024

Table of Contents

Soccer's All-Time Best Women

Marta runs down the field.
She kicks the ball. It's a goal!

Soccer is the most popular sport in the world. The best athletes play for pro teams.

They can also play for their country's team. The World Cup is the top tournament.

INSIDE SOCCER

The first Women's World Cup was in 1991. The US won.

Michelle Akers was a trailblazer in women's soccer. She scored the US team's first ever goal. She scored the most goals in the first Women's World Cup.

10
10

Mia Hamm was famous for scoring goals. She joined the US team when she was 15. She helped the US win two World Cups.

Sun Wen played for China. She had a lot of skills and scored many goals.

INSIDE SOCCER

Michelle Akers and Sun Wen were both named FIFA Player of the Century in 2000.

Birgit Prinz was one of Europe's best players. She helped win two World Cups for Germany.

Birgit Prinz

Abby Wambach helped win a World Cup and two Olympic gold medals for the US. She has scored the most goals for the US team.

Marta was one of the best players ever. She won World Player of the Year six times! She has scored the most World Cup goals of any player.

INSIDE SOCCER

Marta played in six World Cups for Brazil.

Alex Morgan helped win two World Cups for the US. She was one of the team's best scorers. She was a captain for the San Diego Wave.

USA
FIFA Women's World Cup France 2019™

Women's soccer is growing all over the world. Who will the next great players be?

Sam Kerr

Glossary

captain: someone chosen to be a leader for their team

skill: ability that comes from practice

trailblazer: someone who prepares the way for others who follow

Learn More

Calkhoven, Laurie. *Squad Goals: The Unstoppable Women of the US Women's National Soccer Team*. New York: Simon Spotlight, 2023.

Pettman, Kevin. *Women's Soccer Legends 2025*. London: Welbeck, 2025.

Wagner, Zelda. *Soccer Superstars*. Minneapolis: Lerner Publications, 2025.

Index

Photo Acknowledgments

Image credits: Rico Brouwer/Soccrates/Getty Images, p. 5; Brad Smith/USSF/Getty Images, p. 7; Tom Hauck/Getty Images, p. 9; David Madison/Getty Images, p. 11; Ezra Shaw/Allsport/Getty Images, p. 13; Ben Radford/Getty Images, p. 15; Jamie Squire/Getty Images, p. 17 ; Juan Manuel Serrano Arce/Getty Images, p. 19; Alex Grimm/Getty Images, p. 21; Eddie Keogh/The FA via Getty Images, p. 23.
Cover image: Michael Wade/Icon Sportswire via AP Images.
Design elements: vid64/Getty Images; boytaro Thongbun/500px/Getty Images.